April Greiman

LIZ FARRELLY

April Greiman

Floating Ideas into Time and Space

THAMES AND HUDSON

First published in Great Britain
in 1998 by Thames and Hudson Ltd, London

Design copyright © 1998 The Ivy Press

Text copyright © 1998 Liz Farrelly

British Library Cataloguing-in-Publication Data

A catalogue record for this book is
available from the British Library

ISBN 0-500-01866-9

Printed in Hong Kong

Contents

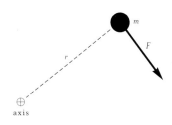

'Thinking about perception. I take perception to mean not only the visual, from a fixed point, but also the connection of the body, the breath, and of multiple perspectives to the symbols around us, as well as their connection to the space of the field where the relationship is activated. Symbols – I include letters here – are not only stand-ins for a concept, or elements in a whole, but things in themselves. For instance, "O" is not only a letter but also something which one can step into, a void, a condition in space that relates to the body; "O" is also related to the breath – when spoken, it hollows the throat, hangs, then evaporates in the air. Different letters and sounds are directly connected to various organ functions in the human body. Likewise, a word can be an image, not merely appended to an "image" to explain it. A sheet of paper isn't merely a neutral receiver of symbols, but a field or space that is traversed. The eye walks, jumps, journeys through, inside and outside of it. It is where relationships are established, not simply communicated.'

April Greiman

Introduction

APRIL GREIMAN, the self-dubbed 'Queen of Chance', is a rare individual in the world of graphic design. Over a 20-year career she has succeeded in exploring strongly held personal beliefs while at the same time attaining commercial success. Greiman is someone who sets her own goals. 'My personal research is about what, in my heart, I feel it is important to explore and discover,' she admits. 'Coincidentally there seem to be clients who are interested in the same type of content.'

Greiman is well known as an early champion of the Apple Macintosh. Her practice of 'hybridizing' various technologies and aesthetics has significantly reconfigured the remit of 'design for communication' by blurring the boundaries between the disparate disciplines of architecture, interior design, and print and motion graphics. Although once labelled as a leading light of the 1980s West Coast 'New Wave', Greiman defies stereotypes by engaging with ideas and concepts way beyond pedestrian design practice. Greiman's designs could be viewed more accurately as 'site specific' to America's 'dream state', infused with the vibrant colours of California's natural environment, informed by the pop and kitsch of Hollywood alongside the ancient cultures of the Pacific Rim, and realized with help from some of Silicon Valley's leading technologists, many of whom are her clients.

Never having touted for work, Greiman found that her reputation spread via word of mouth. The result is a diverse client list that includes fashion houses (Esprit) and fashionable restaurants (Nicola); broadcast and software companies (Lifetime Television, Limbex Corporation); blue-chip telecoms (US West); major cultural institutions (SCI-Arc, the Los Angeles Museum of Contemporary Art); and architectural collaborators (RoTo Architects, Barton Myers). Greiman attained a significant achievement in 1995 when she was asked to design a US postage stamp commemorating the 75th anniversary of women's emancipation.

Lionized by the profession, Greiman has held senior elected roles within the AIGA (American Institute of Graphic Arts) and the AGI (Alliance Graphique Internationale). But over the past few years she has been happier away from the scrutiny of her peer

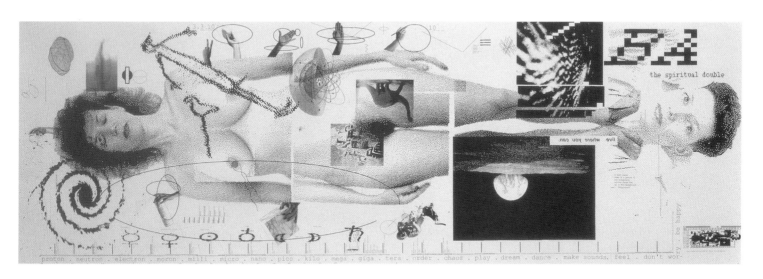

Poster from Design Quarterly No. 133, *'Does it Make Sense?', Walker Art Center, Minneapolis, 1986. Written and designed by April Greiman.*

'Globally, culturally and economically we're moving from working with matter to working with light. With the Macintosh we're manipulating light.'

group and those sections of the design media which fan the flames of partisan resentment between the West and East Coast graphics communities. Greiman prefers to defend the idea of personal expression over adherence to any dogma.

The aspects of Greiman's practice which are truly innovative have little to do with conventional definitions of graphic design. She feeds her left-field stance with her own research and personal agenda, concerned with colour, myth and symbol. As she points out, 'You won't find that taught at any design school.' Championing duality, diversity, abstraction, experimentation and intuition over hard-and-fast rules or predictable solutions, Greiman's animated and dedicated design can be seen as something of a balancing act. In her business life and creative output Greiman dextrously merges various elements – in terms of working methods and image-making tools – into a fluctuating but harmonious whole. Her ability to blend words and images with texture and space, mix technology and science with symbol and myth, as well as combine different creative disciplines, has had a fundamental impact on a profession and art form which, until the 1980s, was informed by one overriding, logic-oriented ideology: Modernism.

Personal approach

In 1990 Greiman published the first book of her work, appropriately titled *Hybrid Imagery: The Fusion of Technology and Graphic Design*. The diversity of techniques gelled into a strong personal approach, and the result was a milestone graphic design publication which assessed the fundamental changes taking place in image-making technology. Six years after the launch of the Macintosh, its implications for graphic design were beginning to be felt and the battle lines were being drawn. Greiman's timely appearance on bookstore shelves, as a pragmatist and visionary rolled into one, guaranteed her a spellbound audience.

Going beyond dogma, even of the postmodern variety, Greiman draws inspiration from many sources. Her practice has been informed and directed by her philosophical readings and by

'I'll always be designing.

It's not what I do, it's who I am.'

Above: 19th Amendment commemorative postage stamp, US Postal Service, 1995.

Left: Billboard for Graphic Design in America, *Walker Art Center travelling exhibition, 1989.*

analysing her own dreams. Although Greiman doesn't practise any particular religion she happily admits to having learnt much about how to live a life from the teachings of Buddha, as well as from Jung and native cultures. When asked about her plans for the future, she reveals the depth of her dedication: 'I'll always be designing. It's not what I do, it's who I am.'

Greiman studied for a BFA (Bachelor of Fine Arts) at Kansas City Art Institute with three European tutors, all graduates of the legendary Basel Design School in Switzerland. It was here that she was introduced to avant-garde European design, and her course was set on the path of experimentation. It was at Kansas, too, that she discovered Jung, in the pages of *Memories, Dreams and Reflections*. 'That book was totally pivotal in my life. Jung talks about his travels, immersing himself in various cultures, and his first experience with Native Americans when he was taught not just to think with his head but also with his heart. Jung has also written some of the most profound books on mythology and symbology.' In 1970 Greiman enrolled in Basel, 'to be closer to the source'.

Greiman's time at Basel marked the beginning of her personal research. 'Basel was completely non-theoretical, a profound education in the perceptual. It was what I call my first experience of Zen because most of the teachers didn't speak English, they taught in silence and body language. Then, for me, the teacher disappeared and I was teaching myself, which was a really invaluable experience.'

Greiman's postgraduate experience provided an understanding of the power of individual sensibilities; it also taught her to recognize when something is complete. 'I believe that all designers come to a task with a unique way of ordering that is particular to their past experiences, and perhaps even their genetic structure. As a student I became aware of these tendencies, and began to trust and develop them. Ideas, hunches and personal visualizations result from that integration between mind and body.'

That knowledge was put to good use when Greiman began to work on the Macintosh, a tool which provides infinite choice, changes and possibilities at the touch of a button. 'I realized that

Posters: From left: '3D, Your Turn, My Turn', Pacific Design Center, Los Angeles, 1983. 'Pacific Wave', Fortuny Museum, Venice, Italy, 1988. 'Making-Thinking',

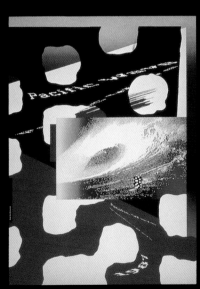

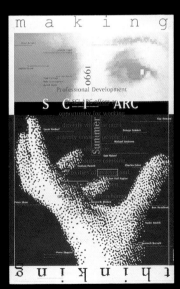

when I couldn't ask any more questions of a design – like: What if this is bigger? – then it's done. Applying that commercially means if something isn't right the night before the deadline, I keep going until I feel I've solved that problem.' Greiman believes that intuition is a kind of non-thinking which cuts through socialization, and is therefore our highest form of intelligence.

The West Coast

'April accidentally moved to Los Angeles in 1976,' is how the biographical notes in Greiman's informal brochure jokingly refer to her major post-Basel shift. She recalls: 'I was born and raised in New York and loved it. But then I came out west, discovered the desert and realized that in LA I could have both extremes – everything I needed from a city as well as peace of mind and total quiet just half an hour away. Not to mention the air quality.' Greiman was enthralled – and profoundly influenced – by the space, scale and colour which she discovered within the supposed 'nothingness' of the Mojave desert.

A chance conversation in LA led to another element falling into place. 'I was complaining about how exhausting it was to have so many dreams. It felt like an incredible resource and a potential education for myself, but I didn't know how to interpret all this information I was receiving. Then I was introduced to Edith Sullwold, who studied at the Jung Institute in Zurich, and for a couple of years she directed me towards research materials and ways to find out more about colour, myth and symbol.' Designers draw inspiration from disparate sources, but to use such personal 'information' for creative inspiration was more akin to the practices of the prewar French Surrealists than any conventional 'problem-solving' strategies. 'If there was a very concrete symbol in a dream I'd sketch it, or I'd write down a word which spoke the loudest. If the symbology was so strong that I'd be in that dream for a couple of weeks, then I'd write the entire dream down so that I would always remember it. After Edith left LA I continued my self-analysis for 15 years. That research became a part of my waking consciousness and daily agenda.'

SCI-Arc, Los Angeles, 1990. SCI-Arc Summer Programs, 1991. Pikes Peak Lithographing Company, Colorado Springs, 1992. SCI-Arc Admissions, 1993.

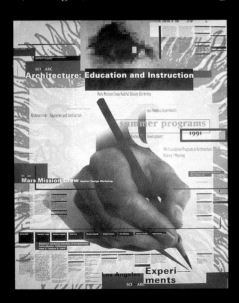

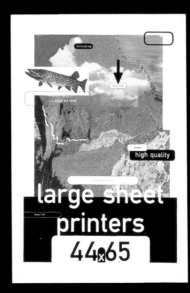

Greiman's research has given her an understanding of signs, symbols, myths and the significance of certain colours. She looks not only at ancient belief systems but also the modern sciences, and has found many overlaps between cultures in her search for 'universal agreement on colours and myths'. Greiman considers that, when used appropriately, colour, myth and symbol add meaning and content to visual communication. Once she's researched a symbol she'll redraw it and incorporate it into any number of projects, effectively adopting it as part of her personal graphic language. Recurring motifs include the Orphic egg (a symbol of transformation and creativity), the phoenix and fire, the golden section and the spiral, alongside the colours of the seven chakras and schematics depicting order, force and matter.

In Los Angeles Greiman located herself, literally, on the wrong side of the tracks, beyond downtown, in a complex of lofts and studios converted from a defunct brewery. Miles from the manicured compounds of LA's media moguls, Greiman's workspace hovers in a no man's land between the city and the encroaching heat, dust and vast skies of the wilderness. This urbane but anti-urban tract of reclaimed industrial space is a fitting site for someone who believes that 'globally, culturally and economically we're moving from working with matter to working with light. With the Macintosh we're manipulating light. Now we've got a global dialogue working on a network of light – the Internet – where we can actually float our ideas, text and images in time and space.'

Experiment and discovery

Greiman's first image-making experiments involved montaging disparate elements generated by hand (paint splatters, torn paper) or photographically (including video images shot from television) and with the aid of whatever technology was around, principally the colour Xerox. She combined this with the creative manipulation of print production processes, mixing four-colour reproduction with duotone, silk-screen and die-cuts on various stock. Greiman's introduction to digital image manipulation came in 1982 when she became Director of the Visual Communications

'All form is content.

So are emotion,

texture, words,

symbols, colour

and technology.'

This page and below opposite: 'Landscapes and textures', experimental images made using an analog computer, Grassvalley synthesizers and live video input, CalArts, Valencia, 1982.

faculty at CalArts (California Institute of the Arts in Valencia, about 55 km/35 miles from LA), and utilized the college's extensive collection of video equipment to make her first electronic 'landscapes' and 'textures'. 'I became disenchanted with print graphics in the early 1980s. Having always been interested in space, scale and time I was a natural to get involved with video.' As an aesthetic pioneer she attracted the attention of the burgeoning video facilities industry and has often been invited to investigate, and demonstrate, the potential of their latest equipment. That way Greiman gets to play with Paintbox, Harry, Henry, Hal and Flame, and the commercial postproduction houses are left with evidence of what their new gadgets can do.

Greiman's introduction to the Apple Macintosh, which fundamentally changed her working methods, came in 1984. 'I went to the first TED [Technology Entertainment Design] conference at the invitation of Harry Marks, the king of motion graphics, who pioneered much of the software used today. He's a genius and a good friend. I was staying at his home and the morning after the wrap party he woke me up saying, "Come on Greiman you're gonna see this little computer which will be perfect for you, we're going to Macy's department store." I reluctantly got dressed, went down to the store and stood in line to use this thing. And for the next hour I completely took it over and pissed everybody off. I found that I could work it without looking at a manual. I got one immediately, an Apple Macintosh with all of 128K memory.'

Greiman sees the computer as 'the real stroke of genius. It's *the* chance tool. You can lose yourself in it and while you think about nothing, intuition takes over.' Far more than a means to an end, 'the computer is the first truly intelligent tool, which means that it's capable of participating in a creative dialogue, and that it's much more than a slave. I've always been a very science-friendly person, but I'm also fascinated by magic and the invisible. That's what is great about this tool – all the real activity is invisible. Something's going on there.'

Resisting any temptation to grow into an anonymous corporate consultancy Greiman has kept her studio small and flexible, with no more than four assistants working there at any one time.

Above: The Greimanski Labs symbol, generated from digital video.

Consequently overheads are low, which allows for down time to become experimental time. She's therefore more likely to take on a project which has scope for self-education rather than one with a hefty fee. 'The studio will hire a new piece of equipment to try it out, or I'll play with some new software if I'm between jobs. I can figure out almost any program by just playing around until I hit on something that looks interesting. I'm definitely the Queen of Chance.' Greiman is happy to stretch the capabilities of the equipment and software she uses.

Reiterating her conviction that the studio is a site for experimentation, and underlining her belief that art and science are simply two sides of the same coin, in 1996 Greiman changed her company name to Greimanski Labs, complete with tongue-in-cheek tag line ('a purely scientific approach') and a promotional T-shirt featuring Einstein. 'He was an artist who just happened to use physics and maths as his mode of expression, and eventually, when we developed finer instruments to test his hunches, he was proved right!'

Form meets content

When it comes to working on a commissioned project Greiman has never had to fulfil a preordained brief, since 'a client will usually ask my advice as to what I think they need'. Consequently this designer supplies 'content' by way of authoring copy, by using still photography and video (which she'll shoot herself or source from her personal archive), and by applying the techniques and programs which she's developed and mastered in the course of her personal research. 'I love to look up the root of a word, especially if I'm working on a logo. I like to emphasize the root or seminal content of a word to tell a story.' Nevertheless, Greiman has been criticized for favouring form over content. She replies with: 'All form is content. So are emotion, texture, words, symbols, colour and technology.'

Greiman's definition of design is all-inclusive. Every piece of design is handled as a three-dimensional object which is affected by, and has an effect on, its context. Her understanding of the relationship between design and context 'started something of a

'Big Fish' poster, Pikes Peak Lithographing Company, 1994. Design and text by April Greiman.

mini-career working with architects on colour and materials palettes'. Her first such commission came from the architect Barton Myers, with whom she designed an identity, signage and colour palette for a major public building, the Cerritos Center for the Performing Arts. 'What I've found with architecture is that there's no faking the scale,' says Greiman. She therefore always tests colours and images in the space before the final installation. At Cerritos this meant painting a large piece of wall and placing it in the foyer to see how colours reacted under various lighting conditions. 'It's part of the fun to scare the hell out of yourself by printing out an image on your nice laser printer and then all of a sudden you're facing it on a 60-foot wall!'

With more recent projects, such as Dorland Mountain Arts Colony in California and Warehouse C in Nagasaki, Greiman has been involved right from the initial concept stage. Her research for such projects is ongoing: 'Whenever I go on a trip, anywhere in the world, I always take a plastic carrying box divided into different compartments, so as to collect all kinds of materials,

vegetation and samples which I may be able to apply to a palette. Of course, when I work on a palette I'll visit the site or the building, but I prefer to be involved right from the planning stage.'

Undaunted by definitions which tightly sanction the role and scope of a graphic designer, Greiman's latest self-initiated project, undertaken in partnership with Michael Rotondi, involves a major shift in focus and lifestyle. The couple have bought a desert motel, Miracle Manor, and aim to live and work, at least part of the time, in this new haven. It comes complete with a hot spring boasting the finest water in the US; in due course clients will be able to 'visit, talk about a project and have a soak, but not necessarily in that order'. Believing as she does in 'checks and balances', and with the aim of 'integrating mind, body and spirit', which has been an ongoing project since her move out west, Greiman is retreating into the desert, away from the distractions of urban life. Giving herself more space and time to lose herself in 'non-thinking', whether within a computer or in nature, may turn up some interesting revelations.

'Whenever I go on a trip, I always take

a plastic carrying box to collect all kinds of

materials, vegetation and samples which

I may be able to apply to a palette.'

Miracle Manor Retreat, Desert Hot Springs, 1998. Pens and ratecards, using photography by Greiman (above), and photograph of inner courtyard (left).

17

MULTIPLE MEDIA

April Greiman communicates across a
multitude of media, from the printed
business card to the Internet site. Working
from the belief that the 'textures' created
by various technologies excite differing
emotions, she mixes and matches
traditional graphic design tools with low-
tech image-making equipment and state-
of-the-art digital image-manipulating
systems. Greiman's earliest projects on
the West Coast were largely print-based
identities and posters for a range of
fashion, entertainment and media clients,
and the magazines *Wet, Main* and
Workspirit. Having discovered the
capabilities of digital image manipulation
she began to apply 'chance' elements,
generated by computers and other time-
and space-based media, across a range
of graphic projects. These included
the comprehensive identity for SCI-Arc,
idents for Lifetime Television and
the logo for Lux Pictures.

m

F

Twisting truth,
revealing secrets,
Digital Image Processing
the sorcerer's
gift.

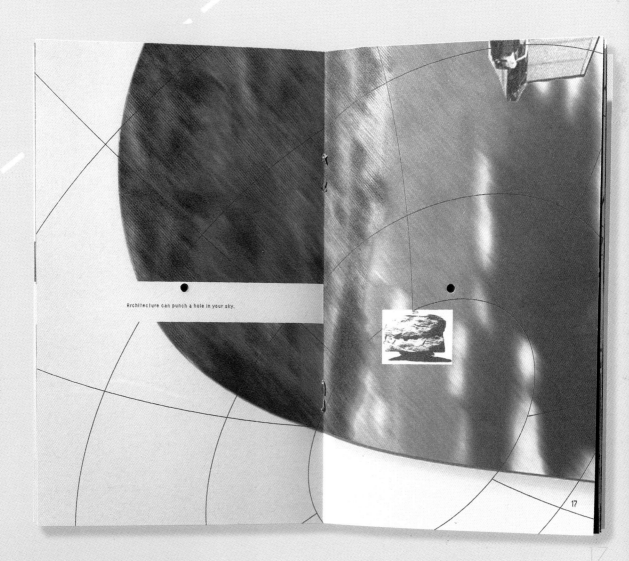

axis

Opposite: Text
screen from Infinite
Illusions: A History of
Computer Graphics
CD-ROM, 1994.

Right: 'Architecture
can punch a hole in
your sky.' Spread from
SCI-Arc Admissions
brochure, 1994.

Architecture can punch a hole in your sky.

Studio identity

'**W**HEN YOU HAVE to print new stationery it always begs the question of whether to reprint the same old thing, or whether you should use the opportunity to say something that's more "of the moment". Graphics are so ephemeral.

'I'd say that the unifying concepts in my own "identity" are humour and symbolism. Appearing on the Web site, and on various types of printed material, are the Orphic egg and a number of funky push animations, alongside the symbols for force, order and matter. The physicist and educator Michael Dobry first showed these to me while we were collaborating on a project called *Inner Architecture*, which was part of an installation called *Digital Campfires* for the Walker Arts Center in Minneapolis. Michael showed me any number of scientific symbols for various ideas, some of which I personally identified with, others of which I slightly modified. I put the symbol for "force" and "order" on my letterhead. Similarly, the image on my studio brochure/folder is an image of a magnetic field which I procured at a computer graphics convention in Japan and later reworked in Photoshop.

'Early in 1997 I adopted a "fictional" company name, Greimanski Labs. I made Greiman into Greimanski and the studio into a lab. Greimanski is a fiction but the labs are a fact. When I needed new stationery I decided to give April Greiman a rest. I'd been using the Greimanski name on my fax form and for my AOL [America On Line] account for over five years, so everyone knows it's me – and my own name still appears on the letterhead. It's just a joke really, but people enjoyed it so much that we registered a DBA ["doing business as"].

'A major function of the studio, since day one, has been as an experimental laboratory for testing out our own ideas. We rent equipment for non-billable work in order to explore what's

STUDIO IDENTITY
Web site graphics, 1998

As a keen technophile Greiman was quick to get on line, back in 1995. Her own Web site showcases recent work and provides links to various clients. The home page features icons, symbols and 'push animations' culled from both personal research and commercial projects. The site can be viewed on *http://www.aprilgreiman.com*.

new in technology and software. Day to day we devote a fair amount of our energies to this process of discovery, especially if we're in between commercial projects. We have an archive of "pure research" images which at a later date may have some direct, or indirect, application. All this research is woven together. Since we have so much parallel processing going on – commercial, applied and pure research projects – with recognizable themes threading through all of it, I think that anything I design is fair game for use as part of our identity. I'm usually involved in developing content with my clients which means that they feel I'm as much the author, and therefore owner, as they are. For instance, when I suggested to Michael that I wanted to use those symbols for my stationery he said "Great!" With the majority of my clients, ownership isn't an issue.'

Restocking the stationery cupboard became an opportunity to design a new identity and adopt the name Greimanski Labs as the studio's 'alter-ego'. Greiman also included a couple of favoured – and telling – scientific symbols on the letterhead.

STUDIO IDENTITY
Scientific symbols, 1994

The physicist and educator Michael Dobry introduced Greiman to a number of scientific symbols which she has since redrawn and incorporated into various projects, including her studio identity. Clockwise from below are the symbols for matter, force and order.

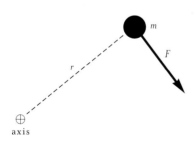

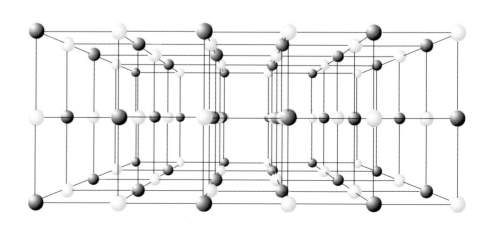

20

April Greiman   Number 211   213 227 1222
620   Los Angeles
Moulton Avenue   California 90031

                                    FAX 213 2278651

Labs

E-MAIL   : Greimanski @ AOL
WWW   : April Greiman.com

>   >

21

IN 1986 ROLF FEHLBAUM came to me wanting to promote his furniture company, Vitra, to an American audience. The name wasn't as well known over here as it was in Europe. Rolf wanted to produce a cultural publication, not simply a product brochure but something that would deal with bigger ideas and include original writing. Being a frequent visitor to the West Coast he'd seen an issue of a magazine called *Main*, which I'd designed, on the theme of "work spirit". *Main* was a trendy, newsprint tabloid published periodically in Venice, California, and he'd picked up a copy when he was making his annual visit to the designer Ray Eames. So he called up and the two of us collaborated on the content, while I developed the logo and the format. We wanted a very informal feel, and opted for paper that was almost newsprint quality. We called the publication *Workspirit*, and I designed the first issue. The content was wide open, and I decided to blend the idea of robotics with a magazine talking about the history and evolution of workspace environments by putting a robot, from Rolf's personal collection, on the cover.

'The Apple Macintosh was crucial to the design process, even though it was still early days in its development. Not only could we design layouts on screen, but we could also reduce a double-page spread to the size of a business card, print out the entire issue and fax it to our team of collaborators, each of whom lived in a different country (the photographer in Italy, the writer in Germany and Rolf in Switzerland). It was the first time I had used low-resolution printouts and the fax machine to communicate with a long-distance client. Rolf never saw the detailed artwork. He supplied the photographs and text and trusted me entirely with making the design decisions.'

WORKSPIRIT
Front and back cover, contents
spread, issue 1, 1986

Working with the furniture company Vitra, Greiman developed the idea of a promotional magazine featuring 'real' content and went on to design the first issue. The front cover (above) **features a low-res scan of a toy robot from Chairman Rolf Fehlbaum's collection.**

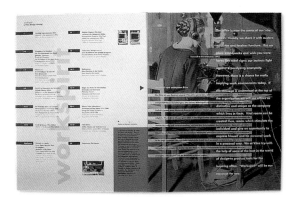

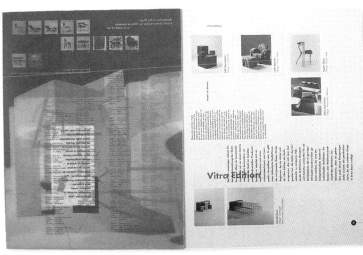

WORKSPIRIT
Spreads, issue 1, 1986

While designing *Workspirit*, Greiman pushed the capabilities of the earliest Apple Macintosh computers to their limit. Here a tracing-paper gatefold is overlaid on a spread illustrating Frank Gehry's Vitra Design Museum.

MARIO BELLINI BROCHURE
Cover and gatefold spreads, 1986

Greiman's design for this product catalogue (also for Fehlbaum and Vitra) reflects the curvaceous, sensual forms of Bellini's furniture. The cover image was blown up and blurred to give it a tactile quality.

'MY FIRST EXPERIENCE of designing motion graphics was on a series of television ads for the clothing company Esprit, when I simply animated a series of out-takes from their still photography campaign. I went on to use a commission from Lifetime Television, to create some five- and ten-second idents, as an opportunity to experiment with a range of new image-making technologies. Working in collaboration with Eric Martin and Bob Engelsiepen, we produced 12 ident spots for the cable channel for the cost of three conventionally produced spots. We managed to stretch the budget by using low-end technology – the Macintosh, Kodak disposable cameras, 8mm video shot on the fly without a tripod – which we "hybridized" together. In other words, I generated all the visuals myself, either in my camera or on my desktop.

'For one spot I drove through the Joshua Tree desert holding a brand-new, just-launched video camera. Then we turned the footage into a total dream sequence. In another spot, which was never aired, the screen was filled with black and white pixelated interference, then a colour bar appeared. The client said that people would think their TVs were broken – and unfortunately they judged it to be too cerebral.

'I used Macromind Director – which at that time was the only motion graphics program for the Macintosh – for story-boarding and for overlaying still images onto live footage. Then we hired postproduction consultants to develop a piece of equipment with which to "bump" the 8mm video footage onto a three-quarter-inch master tape and to transfer images from the Macintosh directly to the Harry, which at the time was the state-of-the-art, broadcast-quality Paintbox. In this way we avoided the financial burden of shooting broadcast-quality video and having to go through all the usual stages, and expenses, of postproduction.'

LIFETIME
TELEVISION
Ident spot, 1987

Greiman used a hand-held camera to shoot video footage of the Californian desert from a moving vehicle. The result combines natural colours and textures with high-speed edginess. The latest digital editing equipment facilitated the split-screen device, enabling various elements to run simultaneously.

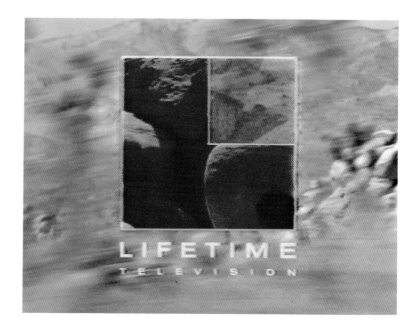

LIFETIME
TFIEVISION
Ident spot, 1987

Experimenting with the potential of the digital pixel – as image, narrative element and metaphor – Greiman created a black and white field of interference which is 'invaded' by a block of 'Lifetime colour'. This ident was considered too radical for US viewers, and was never broadcast.

LIFETIME
TELEVISION
Ident spot, 1987

Using Macromind Director, Greiman was able to add, and animate, a further layer of imagery in postproduction.

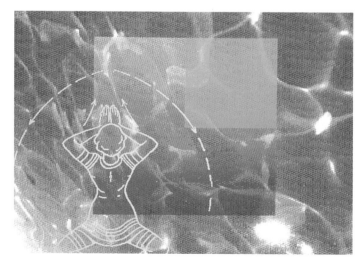

'VE WORKED ON IDENTITY and publishing projects at SCI-Arc, the Southern California Institute of Architecture in Los Angeles, since 1989. I think SCI-Arc probably has the strongest graphic identity of any college in the world. Its overriding value system is not only concerned with how something looks but also with how it feels materially and how it will be used. There's a group-mind at work because this ongoing project is a collaboration between myself, the Director, the Publications and Admissions Directors and whoever needs graphics. We're constantly asking questions about how the school should be communicating and finding ways to integrate new technology. This creates a really good give-and-take situation, and so the messages we create are for the good of the school and don't simply come from one individual. I think that's why the design is so successful.

'My first commission at SCI-Arc was to design the identity. From then on I was responsible for the majority of graphic material produced for the college. They'd been operating since the early 1970s but hadn't adopted a coherent graphic identity, which is typical of many schools and especially architecture colleges. Whoever needed a piece of graphics just designed it, and all their stationery was supplied by an "instant printer". So, to commission a professionally designed identity represented a major commitment.

'I've never had a written brief in my whole career – most of my clients come to me wanting advice as to what they should do. SCI-Arc simply asked me to come up with an identity system for the school. Since they were on the brink of adopting computers – and I was pushing for them to install some as conceptualizing tools – I decided to set myself the task of reflecting their "coming of digital age" in the identity. I chose Zuzana Licko's typeface, Matrix, which at the time was brand new and had been developed specifically for the Macintosh – it was an early "smart" face which was "pixel-efficient" for faster printing.

SCI-ARC
Identity and stationery, 1989

Greiman considers every designed element as an object in space. Her logo and stationery system for SCI-Arc play with massing, space, tension and scale in much the same way that an architect would create diversity within a built form.

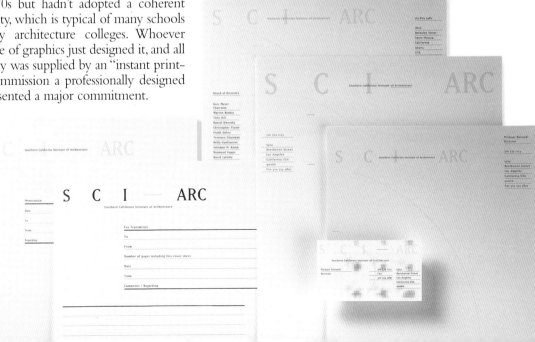

SCI-ARC
Exterior signage, 1994

Over the course of her involvement with SCI-Arc Greiman has mutated and updated the original logo and experimented with its implementation. The free-standing die-cut signage cleverly interacts with the campus context.

SCI-ARC
From the Edge, Student Workbook, 1990
Cover and spreads

This spiral-bound catalogue showcased the work and ideas of SCI-Arc's students. The introductory spreads explore the idea of letterforms as objects in space, resulting in what Greiman terms a 'typographic landscape' on the opening pages *(bottom)*.

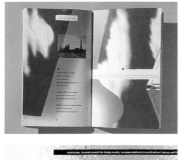

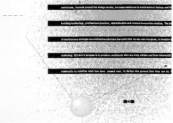

Creating a buzz around SCI-Arc has helped put the college on the map. This is extremely important within an 'industry' – higher education – that has become highly competitive and publicity-conscious. The Admissions brochure uses images shot by Greiman on a low-end still video camera. Note the hole in the cover, 'to represent the void'.

Formally it resembled architecture and I liked its "classical" feel – its square, slab serifs look rather structural, and the capital "I" is like a column.

'I wanted to generate the identity using contemporary ideas and also wanted to "enfold" technology, so I rented time on a Paintbox computer to experiment with space and scale. For me a letterhead is never simply a two-dimensional piece of paper. With the SCI-Arc identity and the letterhead system each of the elements was conceived as an individual space, which was a criterion I imposed on myself.

'A couple of years later, when I was working on SCI-Arc's signage and Web site, I realized that I'd grown tired of the logo. As we'd insisted that everybody use it, it represented a sizeable investment. So we decided to produce a permutation reflecting how the school had evolved. About that time a "tall" version of Matrix was released. I manipulated it to make what I call my first "heavy metal" logo – it was like something for a trendy rock band, an entertainment "flogo" rather than an architecture school logo.

Graphic image, typography and photography are expressively melded in this brochure.

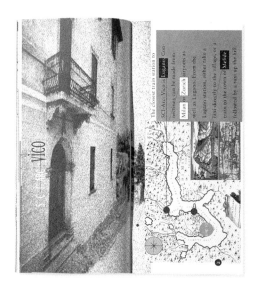

S C I - A R C
Vico, Switzerland,
Graduate programme,
1985–9
Brochure spreads and
fold-down lecture poster

**Material for the Graduate
program brochure pushes
the limits content-wise
while retaining SCI-Arc's
unmistakable '(non)-
corporate' look. For the
brochure, type and image
are layered, inverted,
blocked and cropped,
but presented within a
format common to all
SCI-Arc publications.**

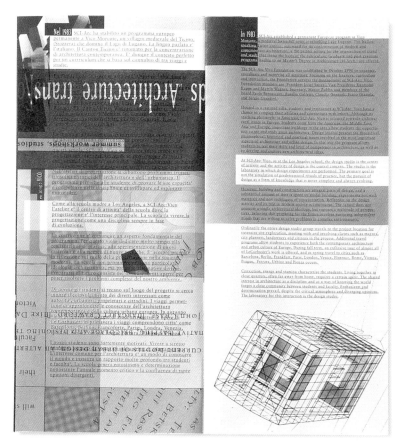

'Anyway, it was very well received, particularly by young potential students and by the newly wired crowd. The identity is still fairly flexible and open to idiosyncratic experimentation. I've always felt that the spirit of an identity should be one of unity, but at the same time there should be diversity – as many different forms of expression as there are voices coming out of the school.

'In 1989 the college hired a Publications Director, Margaret Reeve, and together we suggested projects and generated content. These included the "pizza-box" press kit and shipper, which I proposed in order to house all the material we produced – it can be configured in a number of ways depending on what's inside. We've also designed a series of brochures about special studios and programmes, which have built into a collection of around ten pocket books. They fit into special envelopes which have been tailor-made for the admissions and publications departments, and for the school's public relations firm who send out the brochures as teaser pieces.'

SCI-ARC
Web site home page,
1995

The gravity-defying 'architecture' of the SCI-Arc Web site allows the user to navigate and make links through a mass of information and research, provided by both the students and the faculty.

SCI-ARC
Press kit, 1997

Nicknamed the 'pizza-box', this sturdy mailing container can be reconfigured to accommodate a variety of printed material, posters, publications and tear sheets.

S C I - A R C
Building in LA:
brochure and fold-out
map, 1997
Admissions teaser,
brochure and inserts,
1996
From the Center,
1997

**Greiman collaborates
with both the
Admissions and
Publications Directors
at SCI-Arc.
Consequently the
school's promotional
and academic output
share common
denominators:
they are content-led,
visually appealing and
produced to the highest
standards.** *From the
Center: Design Process
@ SCI-Arc* **features
projects by SCI-Arc
faculty members and
is the follow-up volume
to** *From the Edge.*

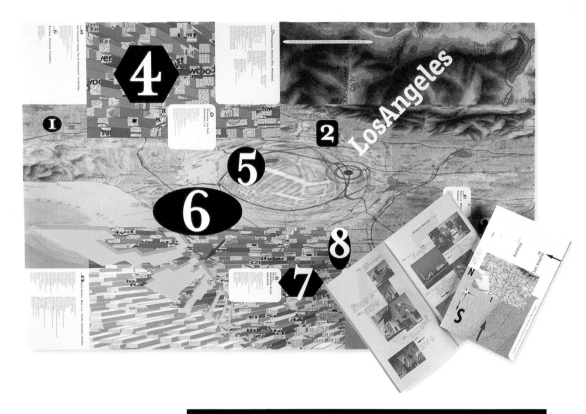

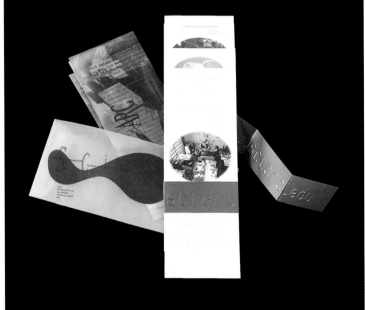

THE EXHIBITION *Urban Revisions: Current Projects for the Public Realm* was held at the Los Angeles Museum of Contemporary Art in 1994. It was curated by Elizabeth Smith and the installation was designed by RoTo Architects. RoTo also helped to develop the content, as the exhibition featured architecture and other projects relating to urban planning. I designed the exhibition catalogue and the theme panels, and suggested how they should be displayed to create a seamless whole. The theme panels were two- and three-dimensional hybrids. They were designed on the Macintosh and contained photographic images, diagrams (which we generated) and typography; but at the same time they were what I call "ephemeral architecture" because of the scale: the sheets of film measured 6 by 10 feet [1.8 by 3 metres]. You can actually look "through" the text and images and see people moving around the exhibition, just like you catch glimpses of people, objects and signs in a real urban environment.

'If content wasn't available we helped to develop it. I thought it would be useful to include diagrams on each theme panel explaining the evolution of cities and of town planning. We looked at the cities of classical Rome, at European cities with definable centres and American cities with multiple districts. We restricted the content to one or two large-scale images per panel, so that the plans and maps would appear "actual size".'

URBAN REVISIONS
Exhibition graphics, MoCA,
Los Angeles, 1994
View of exhibition space *(above)*
and introductory panel *(right)*

**Greiman's 'ephemeral architecture'
presented large-scale reproductions
of architectural and geographic
imagery, mounted on transparent
film. Image, text, structures – and
visitors – were all 'layered' in
'real' time and space.**

URBAN REVISIONS
Exhibition catalogue, 1994

**The layout of this catalogue,
teetering between chaos and
order, closely echoes the 'real
life' exhibition experience.**

32

Urban Re- visions: Current Projects for the Public Realm

During the later 1980s and into the nineties, a number of significant directions have emerged in the fields of city planning and urban design that diverge sharply from patterns of previous thinking about the evolution of cities. These directions include the creation and reclamation of transportation corridors as urban fabrics, the genesis of new neighborhoods oriented to the pedestrian and to public transit in both urban and exurban contexts, a reconsideration of the idea and function of the master plan, and an increasing emphasis on public participation in the planning and design process.

Responding to this thematic framework, URBAN REVISIONS presents a selection of current and recent projects for a variety of primarily North American cities and contexts including Boston; New Haven; New York; Montreal; Raleigh; Des Moines; St. Louis; Portland, Oregon; and Los Angeles. Representing a broad spectrum of theoretical viewpoints, practical applications, and working methodologies, these projects manifest a strong desire to re-think accepted strategies of urban form-giving. Their embodiment of a diverse array of social, cultural, economic, political, technological, and ecological concerns has even in some instances generated a high degree of controversy within the design community and among the general public. Rather than attempting to define a movement, or endorsing one formal or ideological position, URBAN REVISIONS explores a wide range of fresh, responsive, and provocative approaches to the revisioning of cities by some of today's most creative and engaged architects, urban planners, and citizens.

LIMBEX WAS A SOFTWARE company and Web Compass one of their most successful products. I've been working with the people behind Limbex since the early 1980s, when they were called Inference Corporation – I worked on identities, signage, packaging and brochures and did some of my earliest Paintbox work with them, drawing electronic diagrams to illustrate how their programs work. The CEO, Alexander Jacobson, and his VP, Brad Allen, were developing highly specialized software products for artificial intelligence.

'In 1994 they launched an extremely powerful Internet search engine program, Web Compass, and it was actually integrated into the Limbex Web site which I also designed. The main image for Limbex was a satellite photograph of the LA Basin. By double-clicking you could display local information on screen – from traffic maps to weather warnings. It's a constantly searching, self-creating Web site, which was Brad's baby, and is really amazing. He encouraged me to think of the Web as "space", something that you could navigate through, rather than the usual two-dimensional metaphor. So I decided to try transforming the Landsat image into three dimensions. Had Limbex not been bought out by the huge software distribution company, Quarterdeck, I would have included that image in the next version of their Web site. Sadly, it's simply frozen in the space-time coordinates.

'Web Compass itself is an agent for searching databases. It's predominantly used by the business community and is able to bring statistics and analyses to the user while they are working on other documents. We designed an identity for the product packaging and then adapted it for the screen. We also designed graphic icons and elements for the prototype of the Web Compass home page. Unfortunately everything was altered when Limbex was bought out.'

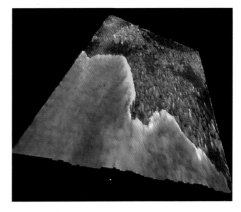

LIMBEX
Web site, 1994
3-D rendering, 1995

The Web site for this software manufacturer incorporates the company's own data-searching product. The 3-D map of the LA Basin was created for an unrealized version of the home page.

help

subjects

rces

documents

resources

agents

bjects

WEB COMPASS
Interface and icons, 1995

Working on this prototype of the Web Compass program, Greiman created a visually sophisticated interface that would run on black and white IBM PCs as well as the more graphics-friendly Apple Mac.

I DESIGNED A PRINT and "motion" identity for Computer Visualizations, a CD-ROM publishing company. The motion ident appears as the opening sequence on every title they publish. I also contributed to *Infinite Illusions: A History of Computer Graphics*, which was intended as a comprehensive archive of the subject featuring over 80 hours of interactive material. We designed the prototype, including the title page, section dividers and text pages, and launched it at Siggraph, the US convention for the computer graphics industry.

'I was hired to do the typographic component but eventually designed an overriding visual concept and a structure for what is a vast amount of material. I generated concepts on the Macintosh which were e-mailed to the publisher in Hawaii. I visited them every month to work with the design team and my collaborator BonOman (who directed the interactive component), together with writer Chris Baker and publisher Richard Childers. I came up with the three-dimensional icons, including the egg, which is a symbol of creativity. We photographed a real egg and "re-illustrated" it on the computer. The egg icon was used for a section on the personalities and studios who were pivotal in the history of computer graphics.'

COMPUTER VISUALIZATIONS
Logo and motion identity, 1994

Highlighting a unique location, this ident features in the opening credits of every CD-ROM produced by the Honolulu-based interactive publishing house.

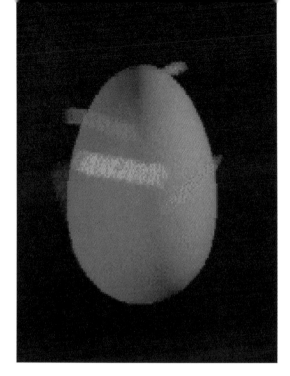

INFINITE
ILLUSIONS
Interactive CD-ROM
prototype, 1994

For this ambitious project, which aimed to chart the evolution of a new medium, Greiman collaborated with in-house design and programming experts who helped translate her moving-graphics palette of symbols, textures, landscapes and edits into icons, text pages and an overall concept.

'A COUPLE OF BRAVE young guys who were starting a motion picture company asked me to design their identity. It's a great name, Lux, and so I made a number of light studies, using video and still photography, which I manipulated in the computer. I then designed two different identity systems, one for Lux Pictures and another for LuxCore, a related partnership that includes a developer and RoTo Architects (who plan to build a new movie and digital media studio). Their Web site includes a typographic "push animation" (a mini-movie activated by double-clicking on an icon), which I designed. I took that as an opportunity to learn to use a new piece of software, After Effects, which is the simplest animation package currently available for the Macintosh. If I can use it, any bozo can!

'US West is one of the USA's largest telecommunications providers. I designed the prototype interface for their Internet product "City Focus", an interactive and comprehensive database of information about a number of major cities.

'If you're planning to visit a new city you simply log on to "City Focus" and type in the city's name; this brings up a series of icons for you to navigate through. Options range from events at major venues to screenings at local cinemas; they also include restaurants organized by type of cuisine. Once you've selected a destination, the program provides details of public transport, road maps and a route. I was hired by the developers, Organics On-Line from San Francisco, as the image designer. Geoff Katz and I collaborated on the concept for the interface, the screens and icons, which meant combining advertising, ticketing capabilities, car rental and hotel reservations with listings, maps and links to other sites. Later an in-house designer put together the thousands of screens.'

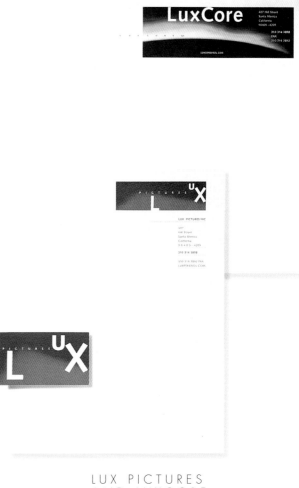

LUX PICTURES
AND LUXCORE
Identities, 1995 and 1996

Emphasizing the 'light' component of these company names, Greiman mixed in ethereal backgrounds culled from personal research. Solid typography was added over these light paintings.

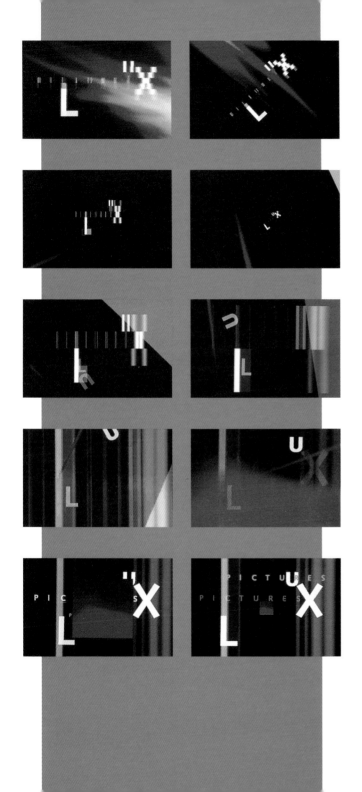

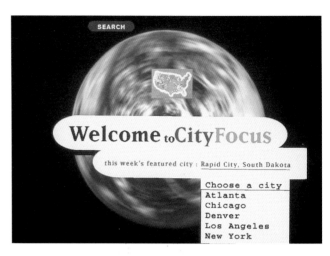

LUX PICTURES
Push animation, 1997

Appropriately for a moving-picture company, the solid type of Lux Pictures' logo fragments and dissolves when animated, veering erratically around and beyond the picture plane. (Images read from top left to bottom right.)

CITY FOCUS
Web site prototype for US West, 1996

The opening sequence for this Web site featured an early 'push animation'. Designing the interface, Greiman 'boxed' the descriptive and decorative elements to aid clarity.

'THE TWO EUROPEAN architects who have had the strongest impact in LA are Richard Neutra and Rudolf Schindler, one of Neutra's young associates from Vienna. Schindler designed some of the area's most interesting architecture but his own house was never completed. A group of architects began to stage seminars and talks there, and the MAK (Museum of Applied Art in Vienna) decided to renovate the building and upgrade the programme, making it an extension of the Austrian museum.

'I've worked on an identity and exhibition graphics for the centre. Mary Jane O'Donnell, the first Programme Director at the Schindler House, was very receptive to ideas. I suggested that the opening invitation should be like a small building, so we produced a die-cut object in a vellum envelope. I was asked to design the identity in the spirit of the original MAK logo and used the typeface Aksidenz Grotesk, a precursor of Univers (used at the MAK in Vienna). It's a lot more quirky, and I combined that with a contemporary face, Orator.

'Another of Schindler's buildings, the Mackey Apartments, has been purchased by the MAK for "artists in residence", mainly thesis students who are invited for six-month residencies. I've designed posters and signage for both buildings, and various templates for graphic material. The MAK Center has many small, infrequent mailings and couldn't afford for me to design everything. But they needed a consistent identity and were keen for their audience instantly to recognize each communication. The solution was a stationery system that included preprinted mastheads which could be overprinted on a laser printer, as and when the events happen. We used kraft paper, which feels non-precious – a spur-of-the-moment communication – with a glorious yellow envelope to complete the kit. The result is an extremely high-quality image, on a budget.'

MAK CENTER @ THE SCHINDLER HOUSE

Opening invitation, 1995
Residence programme
materials, 1995
Havana Project exhibition
poster, 1996

Creating a high-quality image on a tight budget, which would also be sensitive to the overall graphic scheme of the parent museum in Vienna, called for a pragmatic solution spiced with occasional flourishes. The preprinted kraft-paper template functions as an informal and no-nonsense missive. By contrast, the 3-D invitation is a virtuoso piece of 'paper engineering', an art object in miniature. Exhibition posters also provide Greiman with a chance to experiment.

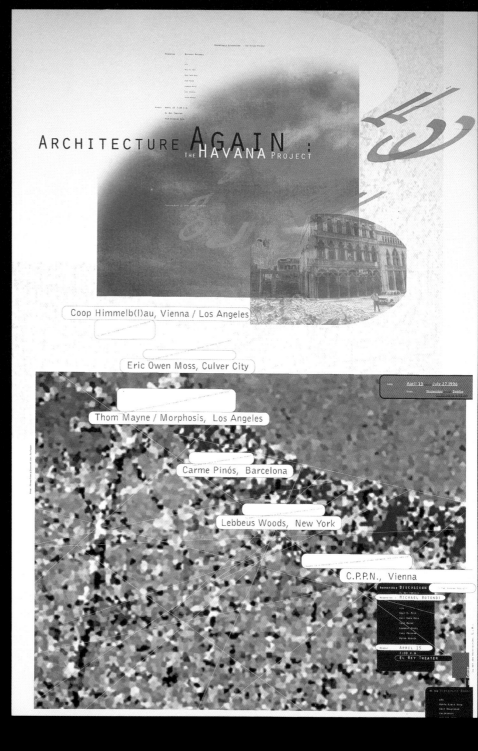

ARCHITECTURE AGAIN : THE HAVANA PROJECT

Coop Himmelb(l)au, Vienna / Los Angeles

Eric Owen Moss, Culver City

Thom Mayne / Morphosis, Los Angeles

Carme Pinós, Barcelona

Lebbeus Woods, New York

C.P.P.N., Vienna

'AN ARCHITECT who graduated from SCI-Arc, I-Ching Tung, was commissioned to design a chain of southern California-style restaurants initially for Taipei, Taiwan. I-Ching had seen what I'd done at Nicola [see page 50] and felt that it perfectly captured the eclectic nature of Californian cuisine. He commissioned me to design a comprehensive identity and wanted the scheme to incorporate floral images, but I didn't want to do this in a strictly literal way. Over the course of the project I-Ching has commissioned a vast range of graphic material for Fresco from business cards, invitations, a wine label and a menu to murals, space dividers and classic monogrammed tableware. We've also done shopping bags, cake boxes and baguette covers for the adjoining delicatessen.'

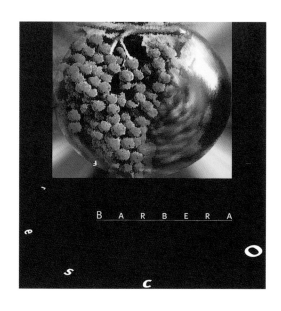

FRESCO
RESTAURANT
Wine label, 1997

A graphic identity based on abstracted images of Californian flora incorporates grapes on this wine label.

FRESCO
RESTAURANT
Dinnerware, 1996

Re-creating the flavour of West Coast America involved sourcing traditional 'diner' dinnerware. Greiman played with the logo while echoing the variety of forms.

FRESCO
RESTAURANT
Graphic identity and
packaging, 1996–7

A vast range of stationery, food packaging, gifts and dinnerware is emblazoned with a flexible identity of abstract shapes and images.

ENVIRONMENTS
PLUS

Greiman begins from the premise that any design project, whether a single piece of stationery or a building which covers an entire city block, should be subject to the same set of considerations. Colour, texture, materials, shape, word and image, scale and space, myth and symbol – all are brought into play because the end result is in effect a three-dimensional object which communicates a message, whatever the scale or medium. Prompted by Greiman's close working relationships with her clients, solutions are negotiable and unrestricted by formal preconceptions. For Greiman a business card is as much an environment as is a Web site or an industrial shed. Such a philosophy puts Greiman in good stead to mediate between the disciplines of graphic design and architecture, and to that effect she has collaborated with architects Barton Myers, RoTo and KMD among others.

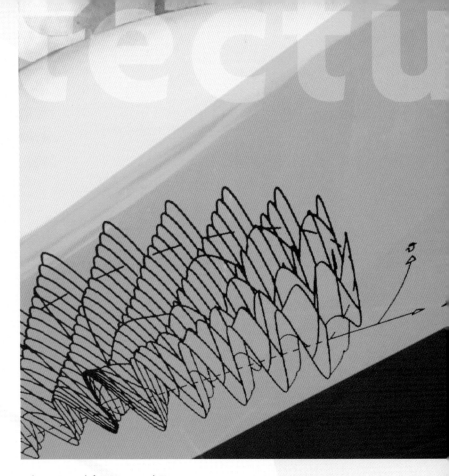

Above: Detail from proposed 'Inner Architecture' interactive installation, Digital Campfires *exhibition, 1994.*

Cerritos Center

'THE CERRITOS CENTER for the Performing Arts in California was my first large-scale "environmental" project. The architect Barton Myers needed someone who could not only work with four-inch square ceramic tiles but also produce a graphic identity and stationery system. He trusted me enough to make the leap from two to three dimensions.

'Initially I was commissioned to design tiled motifs for the four pyramid roofs, and so I borrowed the architectural model and tested out scale and colour combinations. Because the client and architect liked every motif that I showed them, they extended the tiling onto the vaulted roof, certain façades and the bathrooms. Eventually there were a million dollars' worth of tiles on a building of 250,000 square feet [23,000 square metres]. I used three colour palettes, with the exterior palette executed predominantly in tile. For the interior there are two colour schemes using about 35 colours. The public spaces utilize a dramatic palette while the offices and rehearsal rooms have a subtler scheme, sometimes simply a combination of different shades of white.

'The project was begun prior to the launch of Apple's colour Macintosh, so we were cutting out hand-painted squares of paper, making up the motifs and gluing them down. I chose to work with squares because I knew that at some point we would be using the computer, and pixels convert so well into square tiles. Indeed by the time we came to programme and scale the motifs and repeats onto actual applications, the first colour Macintosh had been launched.

CERRITOS CENTER
Graphic identity
and colour palette,
1989–90

Hired because of her experience designing graphic identities applicable to both stationery and signage, Greiman initially produced a series of motifs to be realized in tile *(opposite bottom).* **She eventually coloured and patterned a major part of the building** *(right and opposite top).*

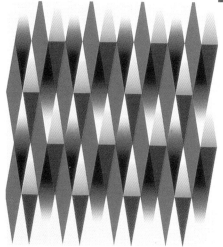

CERRITOS CENTER
Textile design, 1991

Greiman created a geometric pattern on one of the first colour Apple Macs. The furniture company Knoll produced the tapestry textile directly from her disk.

CERRITOS
CENTER
Computer image of
graphic identity, 1989

**The identity for Cerritos
has been reused as the
'icon' for environmental
projects on Greiman's
Web site.**

'Cerritos presented a great opportunity to
play with space and scale. I could take the graduated pattern that we used for the roof tiles,
change the scale on the pattern for the vaulted
roof, and also sand-blast it onto a spiral glass
balustrade. We also took the motifs onto the stationery and programmes, and Knoll wove an
upholstery textile to cover 2,000 auditorium
seats, from a design supplied on a floppy disk.'

CERRITOS
CENTER
Roof tile pattern, 1989
Glass-etched exterior
signage, 1992

**Greiman adapted the
original motifs to create
tiled friezes, inside and out.
The graphic identity was
also etched onto glass.
Amidst all the colour and
pattern there exists an
overall coherence and logic.**

CERRITOS CENTER
Main lobby (with
Barton Myers
Architects), 1993

**This view of the main
entrance highlights
Greiman's interventions
within the interior
scheme, in particular
the glass-etched spiral
balustrade.**

Nicola

'NICOLA SERVES an eclectic mix of South American and Asian cuisines to a predominantly Asian audience, as it's situated in the Japanese Sanwa Bank building (in downtown Los Angeles). I was involved with RoTo Architects on the interior design of the restaurant from day one, collaborating on the materials and finishes. From there came a colour palette and a visual vocabulary for the graphics, based on stone and wood.

'All the wood was ultimately either painted or stained because we had to coat everything with a milky-white fire retardant. It made no sense to use fine woods, so we adopted a natural palette of light ash and a range of colours which I found in bamboo. For the signage and paper products, which included billboards, menus and matchbooks, I took photographs of twigs and pebbles, digitized the images and blended the abstracted "textures" with letterforms. For some of the stationery, I enlarged the image of a tiny piece of wood until it degraded into a mass of different colours and became transformed into a sort of pixelated "forest floor". I designed two versions of the logo: one is a big "N", with or without a circle; in the other, the name "Nicola" reads vertically, as my homage to Asia.'

NICOLA
Graphic identity; colour, finishes and
materials (with RoTo Architects), 1994

**Greiman extrapolated the graphic scheme
from her own photographs of natural
forms and landscapes.**

N I C O L

NICOLA
Mini-billboard, matchboxes and
takeaway food packaging, 1994

**Playing with scale, Greiman shrinks
a landscape onto a matchbox and
enlarges another image until the
pixels resemble the organic
chaos of a forest floor.**

NICOLA
Dinnerware, 1994

**Greiman threw out the graphic
design rule book when she
printed multiple versions of
the Nicola logo onto dinnerware.**

A

'DORLAND MOUNTAIN is the only artists' colony in California. Inland from San Diego, the colony at Temecula has an unusual maritime climate mixed with desert temperatures, which produces an extraordinary variety of vegetation. There are seven cabins at the colony, providing very basic accommodation for artists, musicians and writers who apply to stay there for between one and three months.

'One of the artists' cabins burned to the ground and because they had a very small budget – just the insurance money – the management asked RoTo Architects to recommend a student from SCI-Arc who could design and rebuild the cabin. RoTo decided to work with interns to create it themselves, and I produced the colour palette. Because the building "rose back up after a fire", and since the whole structure is reminiscent of a pyramidal camp fire, I likened it to the phoenix. I chose red roofing tiles and decided to stain the wooden exterior red. I walked around the site collecting sage and other indigenous plants and based the interior colour palette on what I found in the immediate environment.'

'Warehouse C, for the Nagasaki prefecture in Nagasaki harbour, was designed by RoTo Architects; I was responsible for the extremely minimal colour palette. It's a huge building, 108,000 square feet [10,000 square metres], covering an entire city block. The range of colour possibilities was very limited because of the standardized industrial paints the architects were required to use – I could only choose from 17 colours for all the metal components. We decided to leave the Teflon roof structure white to allow more light into the building. The orange sphere, known as "o-sphero" by the locals, is an observation tower. It signifies the rising sun and pinpoints the building from anywhere in the city. I worked with Brian Reiff at RoTo, who produced a computer rendering of the whole building so we could judge the colours "in situ" on the computer.'

DORLAND
MOUNTAIN
ARTS COLONY
Colour palette (with RoTo
Architects), 1995

Inspired by the pyramidal 'campfire' structure and the fire which destroyed the original cabin, Greiman coloured this radical replacement dark red.

WAREHOUSE C
Colour palette (with RoTo
Architects), 1997

**The industrially produced
components for this vast
warehouse were only available in
a restricted colour range. Greiman
adopted an unmissable orange
for the spherical observation
tower, a reference to the rising
sun of the Japanese flag.**

Carlson-Reges Residence

'THE HUSBAND-AND-WIFE team who own the old brewery complex where both myself and RoTo Architects are based, commissioned RoTo to convert a defunct train-switching station into a residence. They asked me to advise on colour, finishes and materials. My idea was to use the colour to articulate the formal and structural massing of the building, so that you'd become more aware of the space.

'In the main living area is a fireplace which you walk through to access the staircase. If it had remained white, as in the architect's model, you wouldn't have recognized that the flue actually wrapped around to become part of the ceiling and a corridor to the second-storey exterior. There are also two structures which form the media room on the second storey, and jut out into the living space. I painted one of them almost-black, or the darkest brown known to man, a colour which I liken to Anubis, the Egyptian god with a dog's head. That form wraps around the ceiling and continues outside onto one of the walkways.

'I wanted the colour palette to reflect the feeling of being in a mountain pass or canyon, because the whole space is so cavernous and vertical, and so I used the colours of lichen. I photographed a collection of lichen from which I chose colour swatches. All the paints were then custom-mixed. The carpet is a dark grey-green which really feels like a blanket of moss, while the kitchen is a very light aqua, which is taken from another actual lichen colour and is quite watery in appearance.'

CARLSON
–REGES
RESIDENCE
Palette of colours,
finishes and materials
(with RoTo Architects),
1996

Greiman likened the exaggerated vertical form of the main space to a canyon, and formulated a colour palette based on a collection of lichen. Architectural forms were painted in distinct colours in order to highlight the interplay of voids and masses.

'AFTER THE LOS ANGELES earthquake in 1994 anumber of public buildings got "red tagged", which meant that certain areas were condemned or had to be structurally upgraded. The Cal State Student Union was one such building.

'I designed 18 banners to hang on flag-poles, and nine vertical banners to cover the façade; I also proposed a tiled mosaic for the plaza behind the building. For that I chose to depict a globe because Cal State is undoubtedly the most international students' union in the US – over 110 native languages are spoken there. Unfortunately the fabrication proved too expensive and the design has not been implemented.

'The building is a nondescript late-1960s construction; with its heavy wood, concrete and glass, it is a hybrid of hippie and institutional architecture. The windows jut out at an angle backed with brick, and extend over six storeys. I was commissioned to design one image that could be cut into nine strips to cover the brick. The resulting image is 40 feet by 60 feet [12 by 18 metres] and contains elements which depict the activities that go on in the building. I also related my colour palette to the architects' primary colour scheme.

'With this sort of project I'll work on the image then test the scale by photographing the proposed site, using Photoshop to paste my designs onto the scanned photographs. Very often I'll alter the design at that point.'

CAL STATE STUDENT UNION
Façade banners, 1997
In situ (computer enhancement)
and the uncut image

Using Photoshop, Greiman abstracted and combined a number of visual elements intended to represent the multiple activities and amenities on offer within the Student Union building – from a game of pool to a film show. The final image was printed on vinyl, sliced into banners and mounted on the façade.

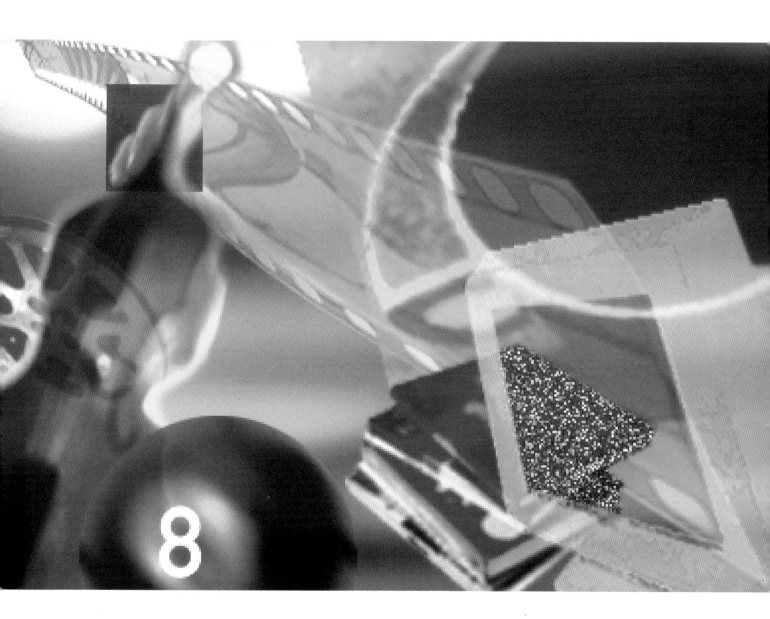

Digital Campfires

'I WAS ASKED TO contribute ideas and designs for an installation to a proposed exhibition at the Walker Arts Center in Minneapolis, called *Digital Campfires*. My concept was to have an interactive display about our physical universe, and so I contacted the physicist and educationalist Michael Dobry, who worked with me on the content. Designed for the large lobby, the interactive installation addresses the user/machine interface and reflects inner space, the lobby as a "site" of passage, escape, expectation and inner architecture. The users, or "players", can choose to explore from these different "secrets of the universe". Their selection is in effect a personal spiritual journey through physics and cosmology.

'The actual interface will consist of nine video screens installed in three caged modules, plus a large display panel outside the museum connected to the modules, so that a number of players can interact at the same time. The interface is controlled by an infrared sensing system and the players interact through hand and body movements – they dance with the computer!

'The inner journey, exploring the uncertain landscapes of the quantum world, will be facilitated by a "fuzzy logic agent" which patterns itself on the responses of the players as they master the events that occur. The agents will teach the users as they play games, such as making an electron change orbit or emerge from a nucleus. The aim is to reveal the mysterious rules of the fundamental forces of the universe.'

INNER ARCHITECTURE
Proposal for *Digital Campfires* exhibition
Walker Arts Center, Minneapolis, 1994

The idea behind this radically interactive exhibit/computer game is to facilitate personal explorations though the mysteries of science and nature. The proposal approximates the screen interface and physical installation of the finished project, which is as yet unrealized. (Background images are of Warehouse C, supplied by RoTo Architects.)

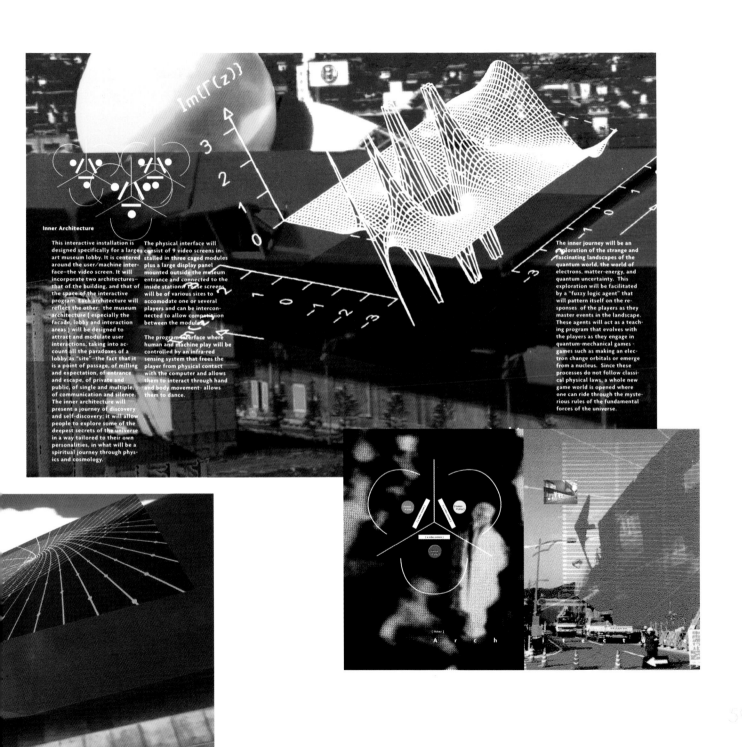

$\text{Im}\{\Gamma(z)\}$

Inner Architecture

This interactive installation is designed specifically for a large art museum lobby. It is centered around the user/machine interface—the video screen. It will incorporate two architectures— that of the building, and that of the space of the interactive program. Each architecture will reflect the other: the museum architecture (especially the facade, lobby and interaction areas) will be designed to attract and modulate user interactions, taking into account all the paradoxes of a lobby as "site"—the fact that it is a point of passage, of milling and expectation, of entrance and escape, of private and public, of single and multiple, of communication and silence. The inner architecture will present a journey of discovery and self-discovery; it will allow people to explore some of the deepest secrets of the universe in a way tailored to their own personalities, in what will be a spiritual journey through physics and cosmology.

The physical interface will consist of 9 video screens installed in three caged modules plus a large display panel mounted outside the museum entrance and connected to the inside stations. These screens will be of various sizes to accomodate one or several players and can be interconnected to allow competition between the modules.

The program interface where human and machine play will be controlled by an infra-red sensing system that frees the player from physical contact with the computer and allows them to interact through hand and body movement- allows them to dance.

The inner journey will be an exploration of the strange and fascinating landscapes of the quantum world, the world of electrons, matter-energy, and quantum uncertainty. This exploration will be facilitated by a "fuzzy logic agent" that will pattern itself on the responses of the players as they master events in the landscape. These agents will act as a teaching program that evolves with the players as they engage in quantum-mechanical games - games such as making an electron change orbitals or emerge from a nucleus. Since these processes do not follow classical physical laws, a whole new game world is opened where one can ride through the mysterious rules of the fundamental forces of the universe.

[Inner]

A r c h i t e c t u

Chronology

1948
Born on Long Island, New York.

1966–70
Studies at Kansas City Art Institute, instructed by teachers from the Allgemeine Kunstgewerbeschule (Design School) in Basel, Switzerland. Graduates with Bachelor of Fine Arts degree (major in Graphic Design, minor in Ceramics).

1970–71
Graduate studies at the Allgemeine Kunstgewerbeschule, Basel.

1975–76
Works with Emilio Ambasz, Curator of Design at Museum of Modern Art (MoMA), New York. Designs graphic materials, signage and environmental work for *The Taxi Project*.

1976
Moves to Los Angeles. Sets up own graphic design studio.

1977
Jayme Odgers kidnaps April to Death Valley.

1981
With photographer Jayme Odgers, one of 16 artists commissioned to design an official poster for the Olympic Games to be staged in Los Angeles in 1984.

1982
Appointed Director of Visual Communications Program at California Institute of the Arts.

1986
Produces issue No.133 of *Design Quarterly* ('Does it Make Sense?'). Develops *Workspirit* magazine for Vitra and designs first issue.

1987
Wins National Endowment for the Arts grant award for computer graphic studies. Awarded Hallmark Fellowship. Produces ident spots for Lifetime Television.

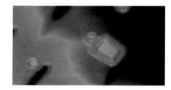

1988
MoMA in New York acquires collection of Greiman's posters. Competition winner in MoMA's *The Modern Poster* exhibition. Grand prize winner at *Mac World*'s first Macintosh Masters Art Contest, in the art category.

1989
Produces billboard and poster for Walker Art Center travelling exhibition, *Graphic Design in America*. One-woman show at Israel Museum, Jerusalem.

Begins working with Southern California Institute of Architecture (SCI-Arc) on identity and publishing projects. April Greiman Inc. is one of three US design firms chosen by the US Information Agency to participate in *Design USA*, an exhibition travelling to the USSR. Begins working on Cerritos Center for the Performing Arts, first large-scale environmental project.

1990
Publication of *Hybrid Imagery: The Fusion of Technology and Graphic Design* (Watson-Guptill, New York) covering Greiman's work over the previous 13 years.

1991
Computer Graphics: April Greiman show at Itoya Gallery, Tokyo.

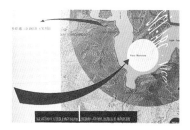

1993
Cerritos Center for the Performing Arts opens.

1994
One-woman exhibition, *It's not what aprilyouthinkitgreimanis*, Arc en Rêve Centre d'Architecture, Bordeaux, France. Catalogue published by Artemis, Zurich. Appointed instructor at SCI-Arc. Produces interior palette (colour, finishes and materials) for Nicola restaurant, Los Angeles. Produces exhibition graphics for *Urban Revisions* exhibition at the Museum of Contemporary Art, Los Angeles. Begins work on interface for Web Compass search engine program.

1995
US Postal Service launches stamp designed by Greiman to commemorate the 19th Amendment. Web Compass interface is awarded Product of the Year at Comdex. Produces colour palette for Dorland Mountain Arts Colony. Begins working on identity and exhibition graphics for MAK Center for Art and Architecture @ the Schindler House, Los Angeles.

1996
Awarded American Institute of Architects (AIA) award for Dorland Mountain Arts Colony (with RoTo Architects). Produces interior palette (colour, finishes and materials) for Carlson–Reges Residence, Los Angeles.

1997
Posters and identities are acquired by the Cooper–Hewitt National Design Museum, New York. Awarded AIA award for colour and finishes at the Carlson–Reges Residence (with RoTo Architects). Produces colour palette for Warehouse C, Nagasaki, Japan. Working with KMD Architects adds 'ephemeral architecture' to CalState Los Angeles Student Union building. Buys Miracle Manor with Michael Rotondi.

1998
Awarded American Institute of Graphic Arts (AIGA) Medal for Innovation.

Index

Acknowledgements

The publishers wish to thank April Greiman and Greimanski Labs for their kind assistance with all aspects of this book.

Photographic credits
Page 15 left: photo Benny Chan
Page 32 top: photo Paula Goldman
Page 48 bottom: photo Tim Street-Porter
Page 49: photo Tim Street-Porter
Page 50 top: photo Assassi Productions
Page 52: photo Assassi Productions
Page 54 top and bottom: photo Benny Chan
Page 55: photo Benny Chan
Page 56: original photo Benny Chan

All photographs courtesy April Greiman.

April Greiman would like to dedicate this little book to Little Rene.

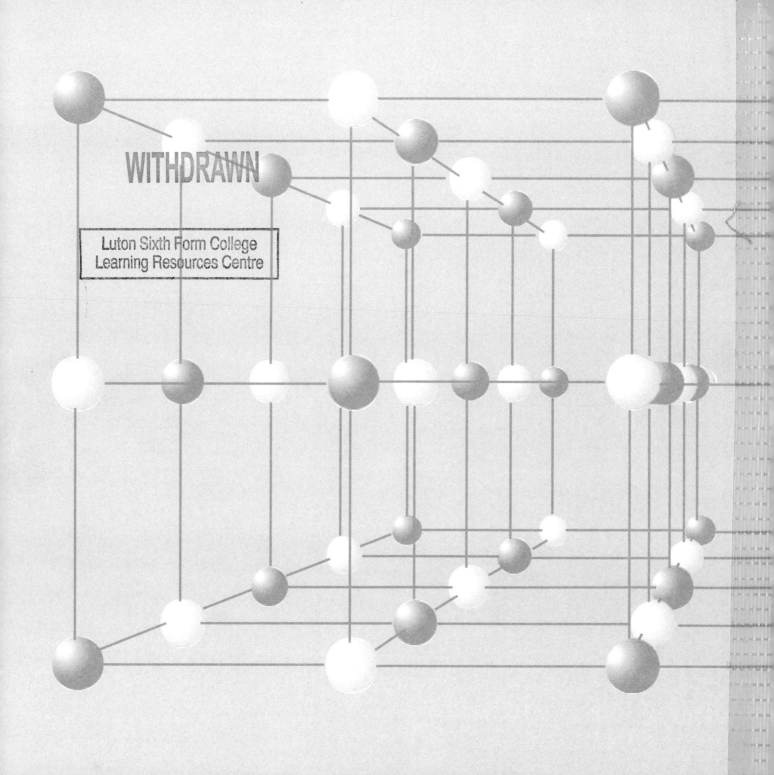